Houghton
Mifflin
Harcourt

CALIFORNIA
JOURNEYS

Program Consultants

Shervaughnna Anderson · Marty Hougen

Carol Jago · Erik Palmer · Shane Templeton

Sheila Valencia · MaryEllen Vogt

Consulting Author · Irene Fountas

Unit 1

Around the Neighborhood

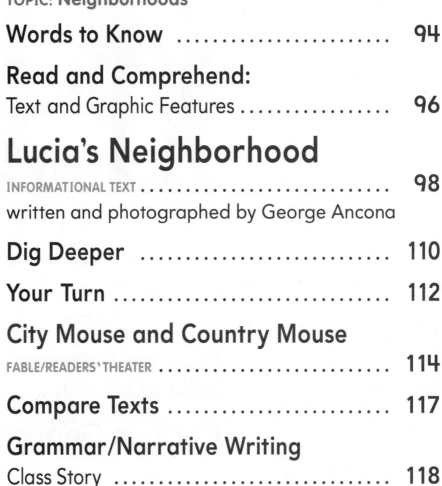

Be a Reading Detective!

Welcome, Reader!

Your help is needed to find clues in texts. As a **Reading Detective**, you will need to **ask lots of questions.** You will also need to **read carefully.**

myNotebook

As you read, mark up the text. Save your work to **myNotebook**.

- Highlight details.
- Add notes and questions.
- Add new words to **myWordList**.

- Use letters and sounds you know to help you read the words.

- Look at the pictures.

- Think about what is happening.

Let's go!

Around the Neighborhood

Stream to Start

❝ The more we get together, the happier we'll be. ❞
— Traditional Song

Performance Task Preview

At the end of this unit, you will write a story. You will be the main character! In your story, you will use details from a text you read in this unit.

hmhfyi.com

Channel One News®

9

Q LANGUAGE DETECTIVE

Talk About Words
Work with a partner.
Use the blue words in
sentences to tell about
something you did.

myNotebook

Add new words to
myWordList. Use them
in your speaking
and writing.

Words to Know

Read
Together

▶ Read each **Context Card**.

▶ Make up a sentence that
uses a blue word.

1 **play**
These pals like to play
in the park.

2 **be**
They like to be on the
same team.

3 and
The children share the paper **and** paint.

4 help
These pals **help** each other wash the dog.

5 with
The boy was in a show **with** his pals.

6 you
I like when **you** play this game with me.

Read Together

Read and Comprehend

☑ **TARGET SKILL**

Main Idea As you read, look for one big idea that the selection is about. This is the **topic**. The **main idea** is the most important idea about the topic. **Details** are bits of information that tell more about the main idea. You can list the main idea and details about a topic on a web like this.

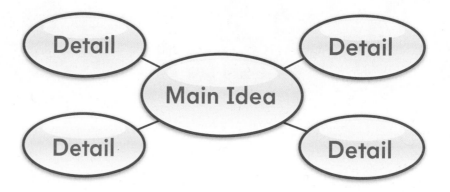

☑ **TARGET STRATEGY**

Summarize Stop to tell important ideas as you read.

ELA RI.1.2, RI.1.10a, SL.1.4, SL.1.5 ELD ELD.PI.1.1, ELD.PI.1.3, ELD.PI.1.6, ELD.PI.1.12a

Friendship

How do pals act?

Pals play together.

They help each other.

Pals take turns.

They are kind.

Pals have fun.

What do you do with your pals?

You will learn all about pals in

What Is a Pal?

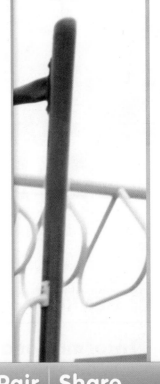

💬 **Think | Draw | Pair | Share**

What is a good pal? Think about it. Draw a picture. Then tell a partner about your picture.

ANCHOR TEXT

✓ GENRE

Informational text tells about things that are real. Look for:

▸ words that tell information

▸ photographs that show details about the real world

Meet the Author and Photographer

Nina Crews

Nina Crews comes from a very creative family. Her parents, Donald Crews and Ann Jonas, are both well-known artists. For her own artwork, Ms. Crews likes to make collages out of photos.

What Is a Pal?

written and photographed by Nina Crews

ESSENTIAL QUESTION

What is important about being a friend?

A pal can help you.

Sam and Nat can help Dan.

A pal can play with you.

Tad, Cam, and Nan can play.

A pal can be a pet.

A pal can be Dad.

A pal can be with you.

A pal is fun to be with!

Are you a pal?

Dig Deeper

Read Together

Use Clues to Analyze the Text

Use these pages to learn about Main Idea and Informational Text. Then read **What Is a Pal?** again.

Main Idea

In **What Is a Pal?**, you read about what it means to be a pal. This is the **topic**. The **main idea** is the most important idea about the topic. What is the main idea? **Details** are bits of information about the main idea. What details did you find out about pals? Use a web to show the main idea and details.

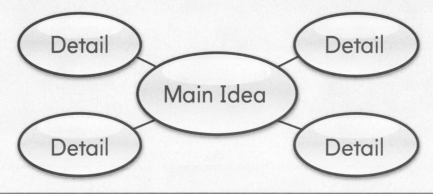

Genre: Informational Text

What Is a Pal? has details that are **facts**. Facts are true information. What facts do you learn from the words?

The pictures show real kids who are pals. What information do you learn from the pictures?

Your Turn

RETURN TO THE ESSENTIAL QUESTION

Turn and Talk

What is important about being a friend? What details does the selection tell about being a pal? What else do you know about being a pal? Tell your partner. Speak in complete sentences.

💬 Classroom Conversation

Talk about these questions with your class.

1. Who could be a pal?

2. What things from **What Is a Pal?** have you done with friends?

3. What words tell about being a good pal?

ELA RI.1.2, W.1.5, SL.1.6 ELD ELD.PI.1.1, ELD.PI.1.3, ELD.PI.1.10, ELD.PI.1.12a

WRITE ABOUT READING

Response Read the last page of the selection again. Write a sentence to answer the question. Draw a picture to go with your answer.

Writing Tip

Read your answer. Add details to give information. Begin your sentence with a capital letter.

POETRY

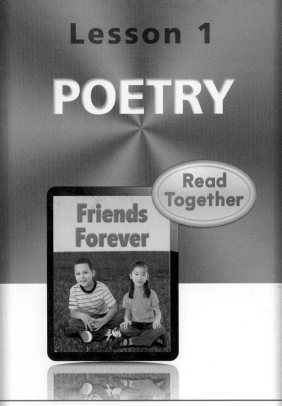

Friends Forever

✔ GENRE

Poetry uses words in interesting ways to show pictures and feelings.

✔ TEXT FOCUS

When words **rhyme,** they end with the same sound, like <u>blue</u> and <u>two</u>. Clap when you <u>hear</u> words that rhyme at the end of the lines.

Friends Forever

How can you be a good friend?
You can play with your friends.
You can share with friends and
help them.

Damon & Blue

Damon & Blue
Just us two
Cruising up the avenue.
You strut, you glide
But mark our stride
Can't beat us when we're
    side by side.

by Nikki Grimes

Wait for Me

Wait for me
and I'll be there
and we'll walk home together,
if it's raining
puddle pails
or if it's sunny weather.

Wait for me
and I'll be there
and we'll walk home together.
You wear red
and I'll wear blue,
and we'll be friends forever.

by Sarah Wilson

Jambo

Jambo Jambo
ambo ambo
mbo mbo
bo bo bo
o o o
bo bo bo
mbo mbo
ambo ambo
Jambo Jambo
HI! HELLO!
Did you Did you
did you know
Jambo means
hello hello!

*by Sundaira
Morninghouse*

Respond to Poetry

- Listen to the poems again. Memorize some lines. Join in!
- Say more rhyming lines that could be added to one of the poems.

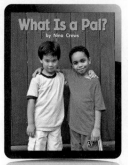

Compare Texts

TEXT TO TEXT

Compare Friends How are the friends in the poems like the pals in the selection? How are they different? Make a chart.

Alike	Different
play help	walk in the rain

TEXT TO SELF

Write Sentences Write sentences to tell your classmates about favorite things you do with your pals.

TEXT TO WORLD

Describing Words Read the poems again. Find words that tell what the friends look like. Find words that tell what they see in their world and show how they feel.

ELA RL.1.4, RI.1.9 ELD ELD.PI.1.1, ELD.PI.1.3, ELD.PI.1.6, ELD.PI.1.7, ELD.PI.1.12a

33

Grammar

Nouns Some words name people or animals. Some words name places or things. Words that name people, animals, places, or things are called **nouns**.

Read Together

Nouns for People

boy

dad

Nouns for Animals

dog

cat

Nouns for Places

house

sky

garden

Nouns for Things

book

door

bed

Talk about each picture with a partner. Name the nouns you see. Then write a noun from the box to name each picture. Use another sheet of paper.

mom   room   city   bird   clock   girl

1.
2.
3.
4.
5.
6.

Connect Grammar to Writing

Share your writing with a partner.
Talk about the nouns you used.

Narrative Writing

Read Together

✓ **Elaboration** Dan drew and wrote about his pals and what they do. Then he thought about what details to add. He added a picture of a ball and a **label**.

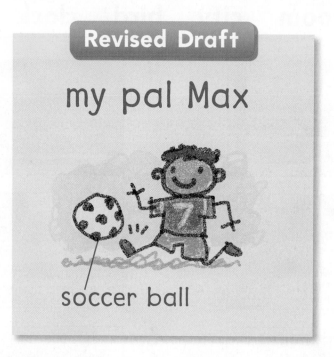

Revised Draft

my pal Max

soccer ball

Writing Checklist

✓ **Elaboration** Does my writing have interesting details about my pals?

✓ Did I use nouns in my labels?

✓ Did I write letters neatly and correctly?

ELA W.1.3, L.1.1a, L.1.1b **ELD** ELD.PI.1.10, ELD.PI.1.12a, ELD.PI.1.12b, ELD.PII.1.4

What do the details in Dan's writing tell you about his pals and what they do? Now revise your writing. Use the Checklist.

Final Copy

My Pals

my mom

van

my brother

computer

my pal Max

soccer ball

Star

rabbit

The Storm
by Raúl Colón

Storms!

Talk About Words
Work with a partner.
Take turns asking and
answering questions
about the photos. Use
the blue words in your
questions and answers.

Words to Know

Read Together

▶ Read each **Context Card**.

▶ Choose two blue words.
Use them in sentences.

1 **he**

He walked across the
street with his friends.

2 **look**

Children look at water
from the fire hose.

ELA RF.1.3g, SL.1.1a, SL.1.2, L.1.1j, L.1.6
ELD ELD.PI.1.1, ELD.PII.1.3a

3 **have**

We have fun seeing the fast fire truck.

4 **for**

The doctor had a kind smile for Ann.

5 **too**

They took hats and the sunblock, too.

6 **what**

What do people do to help you feel safe?

The Storm
by Raúl Colón

Read and Comprehend

☑ **TARGET SKILL**

Understanding Characters The people and animals in a story are the **characters**. Think about who the characters are and what they do. Use story clues, called **text evidence**, to figure out how characters feel and why they act as they do. You can write text evidence in a chart like this.

Characters	Actions

☑ **TARGET STRATEGY**

Infer/Predict Use text evidence to figure out more about the story and to think of what might happen next.

ELA RL.1.3, RL.1.7, RL.1.10a, RL.1.10b, SL.1.1a, SL.1.1c, SL.1.3, SL.1.4 ELD ELD.PI.1.1, ELD.PI.1.3, ELD.PI.1.12a

Weather

How can you tell a storm is coming?

Look at the sky.

Clouds move closer.

What might you hear?

Thunder crashes.

The storm is on its way!

There is some bad weather in the story you will read called **The Storm.**

 Talk About It

What do you know about storms? What would you like to know? Share your ideas with the class. What did you learn from others?

▸ Take turns speaking.

▸ Listen carefully.

▸ Ask questions.

▸ Answer questions.

ANCHOR TEXT

The Storm
by Raúl Colón

Realistic fiction is a made-up story that could happen in real life. Look for:

▶ things that could really happen

▶ people who act like people in real life

Meet the Author and Illustrator

Raúl Colón

As a little boy in Puerto Rico, Raúl Colón was often very sick. He spent a lot of time inside, drawing. He even made his own comic books. Today, Mr. Colón lives in New York and works as an artist and a writer.

The Storm

written and illustrated
by Raúl Colón

ESSENTIAL QUESTION

What happens during
a storm?

Pop has come in.
Look! He is wet.

Tim and Rip ran to him.

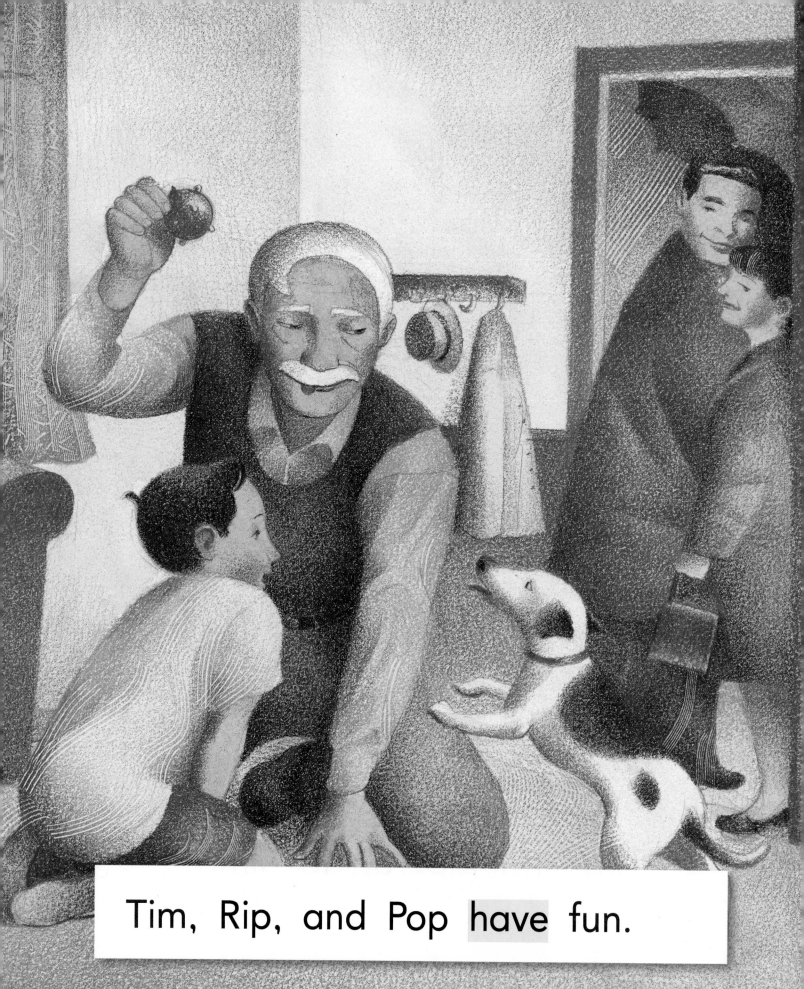

Tim, Rip, and Pop have fun.

Tim had to go to bed.

What did Tim and Rip see?

Tim hid in his bed!
Rip hid, too!

Look what Pop had for Tim.
Tim had a sip.

Pop had a hug for Tim.
He had a hug for Rip, too.

Pop sat with Tim and Rip.

Dig Deeper

Read Together

Use Clues to Analyze the Text

Use these pages to learn more about Understanding Characters and Realistic Fiction. Then read **The Storm** again.

Understanding Characters

In **The Storm**, you read about different **characters**. What important things do the characters do? What does this text evidence tell you about what they are like? Use a chart to list the characters and their actions to help you understand them better.

Characters	Actions

ELA RL.1.3, RL.1.7 ELD ELD.PI.1.6

Genre: Realistic Fiction

The Storm is a story with a beginning, middle, and end. It is a made-up story, but it could happen in real life.

In **realistic fiction**, characters act like real people. The events could really happen. Think about what happens in **The Storm.** Could it happen to you?

Your Turn

RETURN TO THE ESSENTIAL QUESTION

 **Turn and Talk**

What happens during a storm? Talk about what happens during different parts in **The Storm** and how it makes Tim feel. Use words and actions to act out his feelings in a group.

 Classroom Conversation

Talk about these questions with your class.

1 How does Tim show his feelings?

2 How does Pop help Tim?

3 What does Tim see and hear during the storm?

ELA RL.1.3, RL.1.4, RL.1.7, SL.1.4, L.1.5d ELD ELD.PI.1.6, ELD.PI.1.7, ELD.PI.1.8, ELD.PI.1.12a, ELD.PI.1.12b

WRITE ABOUT READING

Response Look at pages 48–49. Write words to tell how Tim feels. Look for text evidence. Use the pictures and the words on the pages to help you.

Writing Tip

Read your answer. Add words that give information.

Read Together

Storms!

☑ **GENRE**

Informational text gives facts on a topic. It can be from a textbook, article, or website. Look for storm facts as you read.

☑ **TEXT FOCUS**

Photographs show pictures of real things with important details. Use these photographs to find out information about storms.

Storms!

A storm is a strong wind with rain or snow. It may have hail or sleet. Warm, light air goes up quickly. It mixes with high, cold air. Look! It's a storm.

This is a lightning storm in Pampa, Texas.

Kinds of Storms

A thunderstorm has thunder and lightning. It can bring heavy rain.

A tornado is a strong, twisting wind. It is shaped like a cone.

A hurricane is a very big storm. It has strong, spinning winds and rain.

A dust storm is a strong wind that carries dust for miles.

rain gauge

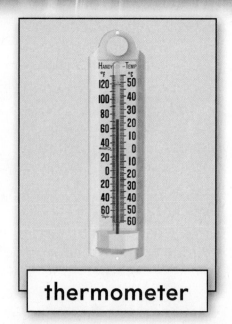

thermometer

wind gauge

wind sock

Measuring Storms

Scientists have tools for measuring storms. They measure heat and cold. They measure the wind. They measure rainfall and snowfall, too.

What storms have you seen?

Compare Texts

Read Together

TEXT TO TEXT

Compare Storms Look again at the selection **Storms!** Talk about each kind of storm. Which kind of storm did Tim and Rip see? Speak one at a time, and listen to everyone's ideas.

TEXT TO SELF

Write Sentences Write about a time you saw a storm. How did the weather change?

TEXT TO WORLD

Connect to Social Studies How can neighbors help each other in a storm? Draw a picture. Tell a partner about it.

ELA RI.1.9, W.1.8, SL.1.1a, SL.1.5 **ELD** ELD.PI.1.1, ELD.PI.1.6, ELD.PI.1.12a

Grammar

Possessive Nouns Some nouns show that one person or one animal owns or has something. These nouns are called **possessive nouns.** They end in **'s.**

Read Together

Possessive Nouns for One Person

a man's hat

one boy's bed

Possessive Nouns for One Animal

a dog's ball

one cat's tail

Talk about each picture with a partner. Tell who has or owns something. Then write a possessive noun from the box to go with each picture. Use another sheet of paper.

| man's | bird's | boy's | dog's | girl's | cat's |

1. a _____ bike

2. a _____ ball

3. a _____ book

4. a _____ food

5. one _____ hat

6. one _____ nest

Connect Grammar to Writing

Share your writing with a partner. Say a sentence with each possessive noun you used.

63

Narrative Writing

☑ **Elaboration** What did Kit's family do at the beach? After the trip, Kit drew and wrote about it. Then she thought of new details. She added a **caption** to explain her picture.

Revised Draft

We saw a fish.

Writing Checklist

☑ **Elaboration** Does my writing have interesting details about my family trip?

☑ Do my captions explain the pictures?

☑ Did I use nouns to name places or things?

ELA W.1.3, W.1.5, L.1.1b ELD ELD.PI.1.10, ELD.PI.1.12a, ELD.PI.1.12b, ELD.PII.1.4

Look for interesting details in Kit's final copy. Then revise your own writing. Use the Checklist.

Final Copy

Our Trip to the Beach

my family

a castle we made

We saw a fish.

We found shells.

Curious George at School
based on Margret and H. A. Rey's Curious George

School Long Ago

🔍 LANGUAGE DETECTIVE

Talk About Words
Work with a partner. Say new sentences with the blue words. Have the sentences tell more about the photos.

Words to Know

Read Together

▶ Read each **Context Card**.

▶ Ask a question that uses one of the blue words.

1 **sing**

These children sing with the music teacher.

2 **do**

The school principal has many things to do.

ELA RF.1.3g, SL.1.4, L.1.1j, L.1.6 **ELD** ELD.PI.1.6, ELD.PII.1.3a

3 they

They like to work together in class.

4 find

The librarian helps children find books.

5 funny

The art teacher drew a funny animal.

6 no

No, you cannot cross until the cars are gone.

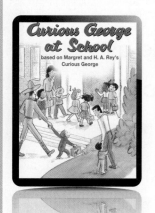

Read Together

Read and Comprehend

Sequence of Events Many stories tell about events in the order in which they happen. This order is called the **sequence of events.** The sequence of events is what happens **first, next,** and **last** in a story. You can use a flow chart like this to write about the events in a story.

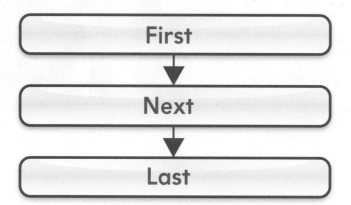

First

↓

Next

↓

Last

☑ **TARGET STRATEGY**

Monitor/Clarify If part of a story doesn't make sense, read that part again.

School

What do children do at school?

They read books.

They sing songs.

They paint and draw.

Children write letters and words.

Read **Curious George at School** to find out what happens at school.

💬 Think | Pair | Share

What do you like to learn about at school? Think about it. Complete the sentences. Then share your answers with a partner.

I like to learn about ___.

___ is more fun than ___.

Learning about ___ makes me feel ___ because ___.

ANCHOR TEXT

Curious George
at School
based on Margret and H. A. Rey's
Curious George

✅ GENRE

A **fantasy** is a story that could not happen in real life. As you read, look for:

▶ events that could not really happen

▶ animals that act like people

Meet the Creators

Margret and H. A. Rey

Children all over the world love Curious George! The Reys' books have been published in Spanish, French, Swedish, Japanese, and many other languages. Since the Reys wrote their first book about the curious little monkey, George has starred in more than 40 books, a TV show, and a movie.

Curious George at School

**based on Margret and H. A. Rey's
Curious George**

ESSENTIAL QUESTION

Why is going to school
important?

This is George.
He can help a lot.

George can sing.
He is funny.

He can see the paints.

Mix, mix, mix a bit.
Mix, mix, mix a lot!

It is a big mess!

George ran.
What did he find?

He got a mop.
He had a big job to do.

No, no!
It is a big, BIG mess!
George is sad, sad, sad.

Kids help him do a big job.
They can help him a lot.
He is not sad!

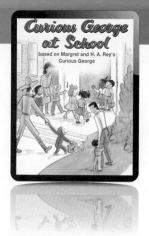

Dig Deeper

Read Together

Use Clues to Analyze the Text

Use these pages to learn more about Sequence of Events and Author's Word Choice. Then read **Curious George at School** again.

Sequence of Events

In **Curious George at School**, you read about what happens to George at school. Authors write what happens in a certain order. Think about what happens **first**, **next**, and **last** as you read. You can use a flow chart to show the order of important events in the story.

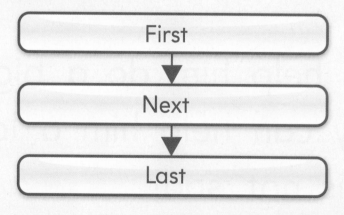

First

↓

Next

↓

Last

ELA RL.1.3 **ELD** ELD.PI.1.6, ELD.PI.1.7, ELD.PI.1.8, ELD.PII.1.2

Author's Word Choice

Writers choose the words they use carefully. Some words help readers picture events. Some words tell more about a character.

The story says that George is funny. What other words does the author use to describe George and the mess he makes?

funny

happy

scared

Your Turn

RETURN TO THE ESSENTIAL QUESTION

 **Turn and Talk**

Why is going to school important? Find text evidence that tells what George learns at school. Tell your partner what happens to him first, next, and last. What do you do at school that is important?

 Classroom Conversation

Talk about these questions with your class.

1 How does George try to help?

2 How do the children help George?

3 How is George's school like your school?

ELA RL.1.2, RL.1.3, RL.1.7, W.1.1, SL.1.4, L.1.6 ELD ELD.PI.1.3, ELD.PI.1.6, ELD.PI.1.11, ELD.PI.1.12a, ELD.PII.1.1, ELD.PII.1.2, ELD.PII.1.6

WRITE ABOUT READING

Response Write sentences to describe George. Tell what you think he is like. Use text evidence to give reasons why you think so.

Use the word **because** when you write reasons for your ideas.

INFORMATIONAL TEXT

Read Together

School
Long Ago

✓ GENRE

Informational text gives facts about a topic. This is a social studies article. Read to find out what the topic is.

✓ TEXT FOCUS

A **chart** is a drawing that lists information in a clear way. What can you learn from the chart on page 88?

School Long Ago

How did children get to school? Was going to school long ago different from going to school today? Let's find out! There were no school buses long ago. Some children had to walk far to get to school.

ELA RI.1.5, RI.1.10 ELD ELD.PI.1.6, ELD.PII.1.1

What did children bring to school?
Long ago, children did not have
backpacks. They carried their
things for school in their arms.
Children did not have a lot
of paper long ago. They
used chalk to write on small
boards called slates.

What did children learn?

Long ago, children learned reading, writing, and math. Some teachers taught children funny songs to sing. What do children learn in school today?

Then	Now

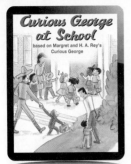

Compare Texts

Read Together

TEXT TO TEXT

Compare Genres Is the story about Curious George real or make-believe? How do you know? Tell how you know **School Long Ago** is true.

TEXT TO SELF

Connect to Experiences Think of something Curious George did that you have also done. Write about it.

TEXT TO WORLD

Draw a Map Draw a map of your classroom. Show where you sit. Describe your classroom to a partner.

ELA RL.1.5, W.1.8 ELD ELD.PI.1.6, ELD.PI.1.12a

Grammar

Action Verbs Some words tell what people and animals do. These action words are called **verbs**.

Read Together

hop

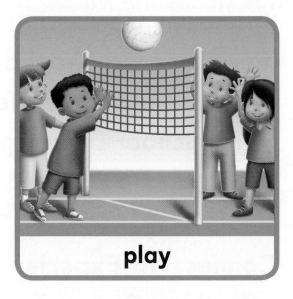
play

jog

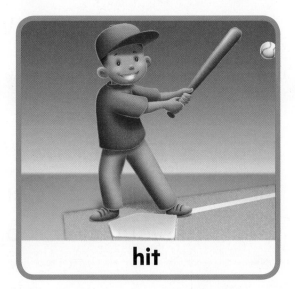
hit

ELA L.1.1e ELD ELD.PII.1.3a

Write a verb from the box to name the action in each picture. Use another sheet of paper. Then act out one of the verbs. Have a partner guess the verb.

paint   help   sip   mix

1.

2.

3.

4.

Connect Grammar to Writing

When you revise your writing, use action verbs to tell about things you do.

Narrative Writing

☑ **Purpose** What things did Leah's class do one day? Leah wrote to tell about the activities her class did. She used action verbs to give readers a clear picture of the events. Leah changed **had** to an action verb that is more exact.

Revised Draft

read
We all ~~had~~ books.
∧

Writing Checklist

☑ **Purpose** Did I write sentences about activities my class did at school?

☑ Did I use action verbs to tell what we did?

☑ Did I write letters neatly and correctly?

☑ Did I write an ending sentence?

Find sentences in Leah's final copy that tell about activities. Find action verbs. Then revise your writing. Use the Checklist.

Fun at School

We all read books.
We wrote stories.
Then we sang songs.
Today was a lot of fun!

Lucia's Neighborhood
by George Ancona

City Mouse and Country Mouse

🔍 LANGUAGE DETECTIVE

Talk About Words
Work with a partner.
Use two of the blue
words in the same
sentence.

Words to Know

Read Together

▶ Read each Context Card.

▶ Tell about a picture,
using the blue word.

1
my
The dentist will check
my teeth.

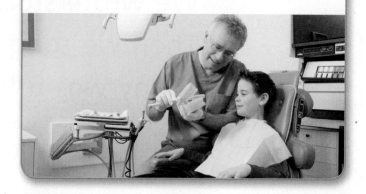

2
here
The firefighters keep
their trucks here.

3

who

Who brings the mail to your house?

4

all

The baker made all of these rolls.

5

does

Does this vet take care of dogs?

6

me

The zookeeper let me pet the koala.

Lucia's Neighborhood
by George Ancona

Read and Comprehend

Read Together

☑ **TARGET SKILL**

Text and Graphic Features Authors may use **special features** like photos, maps, and drawings to explain a topic. Labels and captions can give more information about photos. Use special features to help you get information. You can list the features and the information you learn on a chart.

Feature	Purpose

☑ **TARGET STRATEGY**

Question Ask yourself questions as you read. Look for text evidence to help you answer them.

ELA RI.1.4, RI.1.5, RI.1.10a, SL.1.4, SL.1.6, L.1.1j **ELD** ELD.PI.1.1, ELD.PI.1.3, ELD.PI.1.12a

Neighborhoods

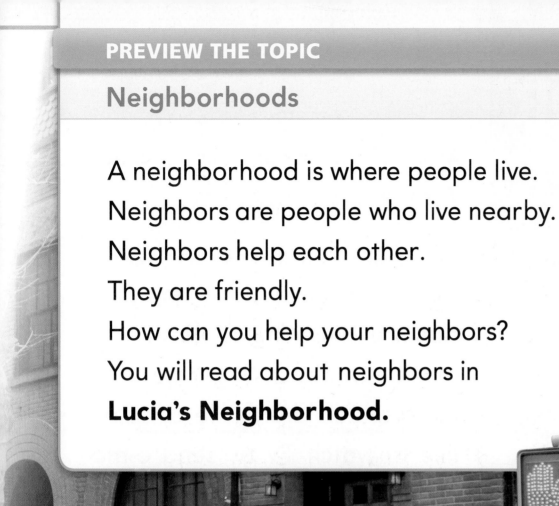

A neighborhood is where people live.

Neighbors are people who live nearby.

Neighbors help each other.

They are friendly.

How can you help your neighbors?

You will read about neighbors in **Lucia's Neighborhood.**

 **Think | Write | Pair | Share**

What do you see in your neighborhood? Think about it. Complete the sentence: I see ____ in my neighborhood. Share with a partner. Act out what you see.

ANCHOR TEXT

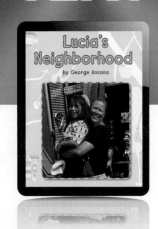

Informational text gives facts about a topic. Look for:

▸ words that tell information

▸ photographs that show details about the real world

Meet the Author and Photographer

George Ancona

What do you like to do for fun? George Ancona enjoys dancing, listening to salsa music, and spending time with his grandchildren. He does not like to watch TV or send e-mail. Mr. Ancona has written many books, including **Mi Música/My Music.**

35

Lucia's Neighborhood

written and photographed by George Ancona

ESSENTIAL QUESTION

Who can you meet in a neighborhood?

Hi! I am Lucia.
Can I get a goal?

Yes! We win.
We all get pins.

Bakery

What can Mom and I do?
Look what we get here.

Pet Shop

I can look at pets here.
It is fun.

Plant Shop

Mom let me get a plant here.
It is not big yet.

Who can fix the street?
Here is the man who can fix it.

Garage

Who can fix a car?
Here is the man who can fix it.

Firehouse

Who has on firefighter's pants?
They are too big to fit me yet!

Library

Does the librarian help me?
Yes!
We sit and look at my book.

My Home

Is it fun to be home?
You bet it is!

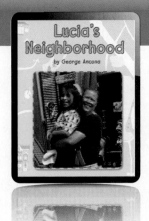

Dig Deeper

Read Together

Use Clues to Analyze the Text

Learn about Text and Graphic Features and Author's Word Choice. Then read **Lucia's Neighborhood** again.

Text and Graphic Features

In **Lucia's Neighborhood,** the author uses special features to tell more about the neighborhood. What information do the photos show? How does each label help you find and understand the information? Use a chart to tell about the special features and the information they give.

Feature	Purpose

Author's Word Choice

An author thinks about what words he or she will use. Choosing certain words or phrases makes the selection fun and interesting to read. Phrases like **on the ball** or **right as rain** are fun ways to say **perfect!**

As you read, ask yourself why the author uses the words he does. Think about what the words really mean.

Your Turn

RETURN TO THE ESSENTIAL QUESTION

 **Turn and Talk**

Who can you meet in a neighborhood? Find text evidence in **Lucia's Neighborhood** to answer. Then draw a picture of a person from your neighborhood. Add a label. Describe the picture to your partner.

 Classroom Conversation

Talk about these questions with your class.

1. What words can you use to tell what Lucia's neighbors are like?

2. How is Lucia's neighborhood like yours?

3. What would you like to ask Lucia about her neighborhood?

 ELA RI.1.7, SL.1.5 ELD ELD.PI.1.1, ELD.PI.1.6, ELD.PI.1.12a

WRITE ABOUT READING

Response Choose one place that Lucia visits. Write sentences that tell what the place is like. Use text evidence, such as the photo and the words on the page, to help you describe the place.

Writing Tip

Begin each sentence with a capital letter. End it with a period.

City Mouse and Country Mouse

Read Together

☑ GENRE

A **fable** is a short story in which a character learns a lesson. The characters in a fable are often animals.

☑ TEXT FOCUS

Fables usually end with a **story lesson**. The lesson is sometimes called a **moral**. Read this fable to find out what lesson the characters learn.

Readers' Theater

City Mouse and Country Mouse

retold by Debbie O'Brien

Cast

Country Mouse

City Mouse

Cat

 Once upon a time, there were two mice.

 I love my country home. Come eat with me.

 I like city food better.

Come with me to the city.
We will eat like kings.

 I will come.

 Here is my home.

 Look at all this yummy food!

 Meow, meow. I will have mice for lunch!

 Who is that?

 It's Cat! Run and hide.

 City Mouse, my home does not have fine food, but it is safe. I'm going back to the country.

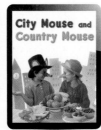

Compare Texts

TEXT TO TEXT

Compare Feelings How do Lucia and the mice feel about their neighborhoods? How do you know?

TEXT TO SELF

Respond to the Story What lesson does Country Mouse learn? Has anything like this ever happened to you? Write sentences about it.

TEXT TO WORLD

Discuss Neighborhoods Who or what makes your neighborhood special? Describe to a partner. Use details.

ELA RL.1.2, RL.1.9, RI.1.9, W.1.8, SL.1.4 ELD ELD.PI.1.6, ELD.PI.1.11, ELD.PI.1.12a

Grammar

Adjectives Some words describe people, animals, places, or things. These describing words are called **adjectives**. Adjectives can describe by telling size or shape.

Read Together

Adjectives for Size

tall

long

short

tiny

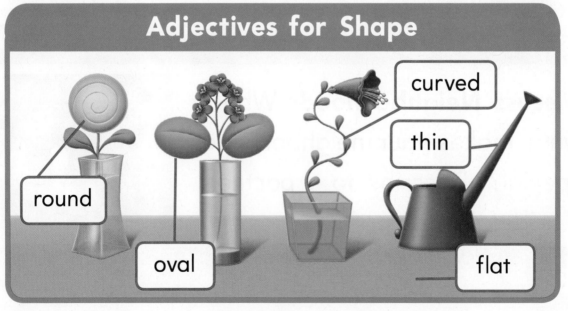

Adjectives for Shape

curved

thin

round

oval

flat

ELA L.1.1f ELD ELD.PII.1.4, ELD.PII.1.5

Try This!

Think of an adjective for size or shape to describe each picture. Write the word on another sheet of paper. Use the adjective in a sentence.

1.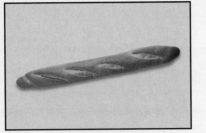

2.

3.

4.

5.

Connect Grammar to Writing

When you revise your class story, look for places to add adjectives to tell what things look like.

Narrative Writing

✓ **Elaboration** When you write a **class story**, choose interesting words that are just right!

Ms. Soto's class wrote about their town. Later, they changed **big** to a clearer word.

Revised Draft

Our town has a big parade.

Funny clowns wear ~~big~~ tall hats.

Revising Checklist

- ✓ Does our story have interesting details?
- ✓ Did we use nouns that are exact?
- ✓ Did we use adjectives to tell about size or shape?
- ✓ Did we write a sentence to end the story?

ELA W.1.3, W.1.5, L.1.1b, L.1.1f ELD ELD.PI.1.10, ELD.PI.1.12a, ELD.PI.1.12b, ELD.PII.1.4, ELD.PII.1.5

Read the story that Ms. Soto's class wrote. Find adjectives that tell about size and shape. Now help revise your class story. Use the Checklist.

Final Copy

Our Town Parade

Our town has a big parade.
Funny clowns wear tall hats.
A fire truck blasts its horn.
Horses prance down wide streets.
At the end, a loud band marches by.

Gus Takes the Train
by Russell Benfanti

City Zoo

🔍 LANGUAGE DETECTIVE

Talk About Words
Verbs are words that tell what people and animals do. Work with a partner. Find the blue words that are verbs. Use them in sentences.

Words to Know

Read Together

▶ Read each **Context Card**.

▶ Use a blue word to tell about something you did.

1 **many**

There are **many** cars on the street.

2 **friend**

She likes to ride the bus with her **friend**.

ELA RF.1.3g, L.1.1e, L.1.6 **ELD** ELD.PI.1.1, ELD.PI.1.12a, ELD.PII.1.3a, ELD.PII.1.3b

3 full

This train is always **full** of people.

4 pull

He can **pull** his pet in the wagon.

5 hold

She can **hold** her phone in her hand.

6 good

The ferry is a **good** way to see the city.

Read and Comprehend

Read Together

☑ **TARGET SKILL**

Story Structure A story has different parts. The **characters** are the people and animals in a story. The **setting** is when and where it takes place. The **plot** is the story events. It is the problem the characters have and how they solve it. You can use a story map to tell who is in a story, where they are, and what they do.

Characters	Setting
Plot	

☑ **TARGET STRATEGY**

Analyze/Evaluate Tell what you think of the story. Give text evidence to tell why.

ELA RL.1.3, RL.1.10a, SL.1.4, SL.1.6 ELD ELD.PI.1.1, ELD.PI.1.3, ELD.PI.1.6, ELD.PI.1.12a

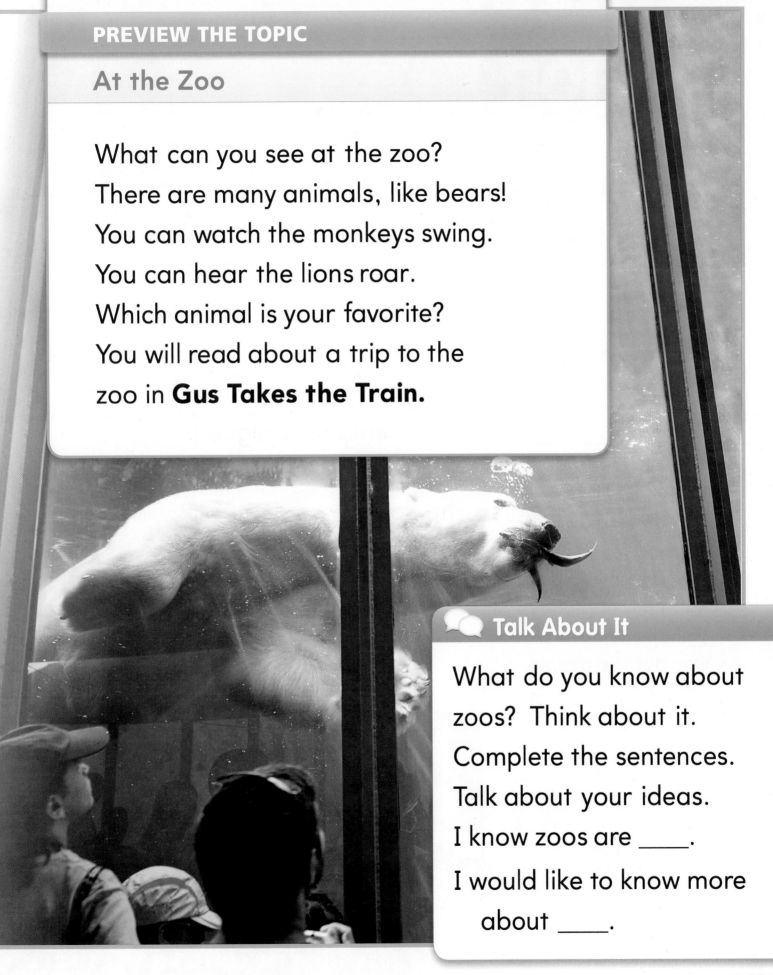

At the Zoo

What can you see at the zoo?
There are many animals, like bears!
You can watch the monkeys swing.
You can hear the lions roar.
Which animal is your favorite?
You will read about a trip to the
zoo in **Gus Takes the Train.**

💬 Talk About It

What do you know about
zoos? Think about it.
Complete the sentences.
Talk about your ideas.
I know zoos are ____.
I would like to know more
about ____.

ANCHOR TEXT

Gus Takes the Train
by Russell Benfanti

✅ **GENRE**

A **fantasy** is a story that could not happen in real life. As you read, look for:

▸ events that could not really happen
▸ animal characters who act like people

Meet the Author and Illustrator

Russell Benfanti

If you like Russell Benfanti's colorful artwork, then visit a toy store. There you will find board games, toy packages, and computer games that Mr. Benfanti designed. "I love what I do!" he says.

Gus Takes the Train

written and illustrated by Russell Benfanti

ESSENTIAL QUESTION

What happens
on the train?

Gus has to run to get the train.
He has a big bag to pull.

Run, Gus, run!

Gus cannot pull up his bag.
The conductor can help him.

The train is full.
Gus can see many kids.

Gus sat.

His big bag can go up here.

Gus met a friend!
Peg and Gus sing and play.

Peg can hold the cups for Gus.
They are too full!

Peg and Gus have a sip.
It is good!

Gus can see a lot.
A funny bug is on the window!

We are here!
Gus had fun on the train.

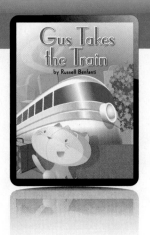

Dig Deeper

Read Together

Use Clues to Analyze the Text

Use these pages to learn more about
Story Structure and Fantasy. Then read
Gus Takes the Train again.

Story Structure

Gus Takes the Train has **characters**,
settings, and a **plot**. All of these work
together to tell the story. Who are the
characters? Where are they in different
parts of the story? Write text evidence on
a story map to tell who is in the story,
where they are, and what they do.

Characters	Settings
Plot	

Genre: Fantasy

This story is a **fantasy**. That means it is make-believe and could not happen in real life. In the story, Gus sings. Can cats sing a song in real life?

Look again at the pictures in the story. Do they look like real life? What text evidence tells you that this story is a fantasy?

Your Turn

RETURN TO THE ESSENTIAL QUESTION

 **Turn and Talk**

What happens on the train? Tell what Gus does first, next, and last. Then draw a picture of something Gus will see at the zoo. Describe it. Show your picture as you talk to help explain your ideas.

 Classroom Conversation

Talk about these questions with your class.

1 Why does Gus take the train?

2 How does Peg help Gus?

3 Think about the end of the story. What will Gus do next?

WRITE ABOUT READING ··································

Response Write the story the way Peg would tell it. Write sentences to tell what happens at the beginning, middle, and end of the story.

Writing Tip

Add words like **first, next,** and **last** to tell when things happen.

INFORMATIONAL TEXT

Read Together

✓ GENRE

Informational text gives facts about a topic. It can be from a magazine, brochure, or website. What is the topic of this selection?

✓ TEXT FOCUS

A **map** is a drawing of a place. It can help you to get somewhere. A **key** shows what pictures on the map mean. What does each picture in the key on page 143 mean?

City Zoo

Welcome to the City Zoo! The zoo is full of many interesting animals. See if you can find all the animals on the map.

Key

tiger

elephant

polar bear

giraffe

We hope you have a good time at the zoo.

- Come with your family and a friend.

- Hold on to your ticket.

- Have some snacks.

- Pull a wagon.

- Take pictures.

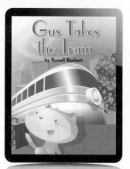
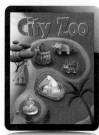

Compare Texts

TEXT TO TEXT

Compare Selections Think about both selections. Tell which is make-believe and which is true. Tell how you know.

TEXT TO SELF

Give Directions Write to tell how you would get to one of the animals at the zoo. Then use the map, and show and tell your classmates how you got there.

TEXT TO WORLD

Connect to Social Studies Imagine that you are traveling to study animals. Where would you go? Find that place on a map or globe. Describe your trip. Use details.

ELA RL.1.5, SL.1.2a, SL.1.4 ELD ELD.PI.1.6, ELD.PI.1.9, ELD.PII.1.6

Grammar

Adjectives Some **adjectives** describe people, animals, places, or things by telling their color or how many.

Read Together

Adjectives for Color

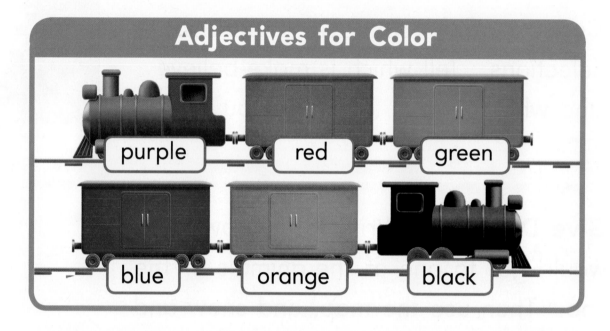

purple   red   green

blue   orange   black

Adjectives for Number

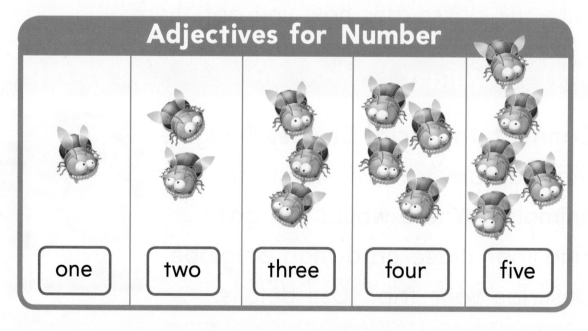

one   two   three   four   five

146   ELA L.1.1f   ELD ELD.PII.1.4

Write one number adjective and one color adjective to describe each item. Talk with your partner about how adjectives help tell what things are like.

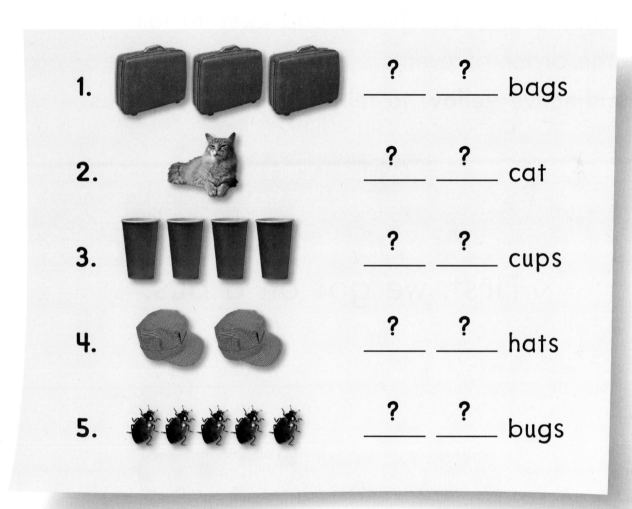

1. __?__ __?__ bags

2. __?__ __?__ cat

3. __?__ __?__ cups

4. __?__ __?__ hats

5. __?__ __?__ bugs

Connect Grammar to Writing

When you revise your writing, look for places where you can add adjectives to tell what things are like.

Narrative Writing

☑ **Elaboration** When you write a **class story**, use adjectives to describe things clearly.

Mr. Tam's class wrote about a bus trip. They used **First, Next,** and **Last** to tell the order of events. Then they added the adjective **yellow** to tell more about the bus.

Revised Draft

First, we got on a yellow bus.

Revising Checklist

☑ Are the story events in the correct order?

☑ Did we use words like **First, Next,** and **Last** to show the order?

☑ Could we tell more by adding adjectives?

Final Copy

A City Bus Ride

Our class took a bus trip.
First, we got on a yellow bus.
Next, we sang two songs.
Last, we saw tall buildings and
long trains.
We had fun on our class trip.

Write a Story

Read
Together

TASK Look at **Lucia's Neighborhood.** What would you like to do in Lucia's neighborhood? What places in the neighborhood would you like to see? Write a story to tell classmates about having fun in Lucia's neighborhood.

PLAN · ▤ myNotebook

Gather Information Talk with a group about **Lucia's Neighborhood.** Where does Lucia go? What does she do?

Use the tools in your eBook to remember facts about Lucia and where she lives.

Write your story ideas in a story map.

- Who will be in your story?

- Where will you go?

- What will you do?

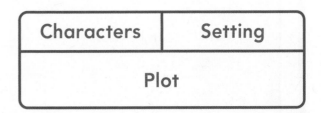

Characters	Setting
Plot	

 ELA W.1.3, W.1.5, W.1.6, W.1.8, SL.1.4, SL.1.5, L.1.1f, L.1.1j, L.1.2b ELD ELD.PI.1.1, ELD.PI.1.10, ELD.PI.1.12b, ELD.PII.1.1, ELD.PII.1.2, ELD.PII.1.3a, ELD.PII.1.4

Write your draft in *my*WriteSmart.

Write Your Story Use your story map for ideas. Follow these steps.

First

Begin your story. Who is with you in Lucia's neighborhood? Where do you go? Write a sentence that tells the first thing you do.

First, _____.

Next

What happens next? Write a sentence to tell about it. Use action verbs and adjectives to help you explain.

Next, _____.

Last

Write a sentence to tell the last event.

Last, _____.

Ending

Give your story a nice ending. Use one of these ideas or your own idea.

- Tell how your visit made you feel.
- Tell about the best part of your visit.

Review Your Draft Read your writing and make it better. Use the Checklist.

- ☑ Is my story about how I have fun in Lucia's neighborhood?

- ☑ Did I use **first**, **next**, and **last** to show the order of events?

- ☑ Did I use action verbs and adjectives to help explain what happens?

- ☑ Does each sentence begin with a capital letter and end with a period?

my WriteSmart

Ask a partner to read your draft. Talk about how you can make it better.

PRESENT

Share Make a final copy of your story. Add a picture. Pick a way to share.

- Read your story to a group.

- Put your story in a class book.

We Go to Lucia's Neighborhood

Unit 1 High-Frequency Words

❶ What Is a Pal?

play
be
and
help
with
you

❷ The Storm

he
look
have
for
too
what

❸ Curious George at School

sing
do
they
find
no
funny

❹ Lucia's Neighborhood

my
here
who
all
does
me

❺ Gus Takes the Train

many
friend
full
pull
hold
good

B

bed

A **bed** is a kind of furniture for sleeping.
I sleep in my **bed**.

book

A **book** is a group of pages with words on them.
Frog and Toad is my favorite **book**.

C

car

A **car** is a machine with four wheels. We go in a **car** to visit my grandparents.

come

To **come** means to move toward something.
Maria called the puppy to **come** to her.

conductor

The **conductor** is the person in charge of a train. The train **conductor** watched the tracks closely.

curious

To be **curious** is to want to learn. Alan was **curious** about dinosaurs.

F

firefighter's

A **firefighter** is someone who puts out fires. A **firefighter's** job can be dangerous.

fun

To have **fun** is to have a good time. The children had **fun** playing tag.

G

George

George is a boy's name. My son's name is **George**.

goal

A **goal** is a score in a game. Anita kicked the ball and made a **goal**.

H

hi

The word **hi** means hello. I say **hi** when I see someone I know.

home

A **home** is a place where people or animals live. There are six people living in my **home**.

J

job

A **job** is work for people to do. Uncle Ned has a **job** in a store.

K

kids

Kid is another word for child.
My uncle tells funny stories about
when he and my dad were **kids**.

L

librarian

A **librarian** works in a place where many books are kept.
The **librarian** helped me find the book I was looking for.

Lucia

Lucia is a girl's name. My sister's name is **Lucia**.

M

mess

A **mess** is something that is not neat. My sister's room
is a **mess!**

N

neighborhood

A **neighborhood** is a part of a city or town.
Jim walks to the store in his **neighborhood**.

P

paints

Paints are liquids with colors in them.
Dip the big brushes into the **paints**.

pal

A **pal** is a friend. Benny is
my best **pal**.

pants

People wear **pants** over their legs.
Lucy's **pants** have two big pockets.

pet

A **pet** is an animal who lives with you.
My cat Sam is the best **pet** ever!

plant

A **plant** is anything alive that is not a person or an animal. We have a **plant** with big green leaves in our kitchen.

Pop

Pop is one name for a grandfather. I call my mother's father **Pop**.

S

school

A **school** is a place where students learn from teachers. I learn to read at **school**.

storm

A **storm** is strong wind, rain, or snow. Lots of rain fell during the **storm**.

street

A **street** is a road in a city or a town. We live on a very busy **street**.

T

takes

The word **takes** can mean to travel by.
Mia **takes** the bus to school.

this

This means something that is near you.
This is the book I'm taking home.

train

A **train** is a group of railroad
cars. This summer my family
is going on a **train** ride.

W

wet

Wet means covered with liquid. Juan got **wet** when he went out in the rain.

what

The word **what** is used to ask questions. **What** did you eat for breakfast?

window

A **window** is an open place in a wall. Sasha opened the **window.**

Acknowledgments

Curious George at School, text by Houghton Mifflin Harcourt Publishing, illustrated by Margret and H.A. Rey. Copyright ©2011 by Houghton Mifflin Harcourt Publishing Company. All rights reserved. The character Curious George® including without limitation the character's name and the character's likeness are registered trademarks of Houghton Mifflin Harcourt Publishing Company. Curious George logo is a trademark of Houghton Mifflin Harcourt Publishing Company.

"Damon & Blue" from *My Man Blue* by Nikki Grimes. Copyright ©1999 by Nikki Grimes. Reprinted by permission of Dial Books for Young Readers, a division of Penguin Young Readers Group, a member of Penguin Group (USA) Inc., 345 Hudson Street, New York, NY 10014 and Curtis Brown, Ltd.

"Jambo" from *Nightfeathers* by Sundaira Morninghouse. Copyright ©1989 by Sundaira Morninghouse. Reprinted by permission of Open Hand Publishing, LLC (www.openhand.com).

"Wait for Me" by Sarah Wilson from *June Is a Tune That Jumps on a Stair*. Copyright ©1992 by Sarah Wilson. Reprinted by permission of the author.

Credits

Placement Key:

(r) right, (l) left, (c) center, (t) top, (b) bottom, (bg) background

Photo Credits

3 (cl) © Rommel/Masterfile; **3** (bl) ©Colin Hogan/Alamy; **4** (bl) © Douglas Keister/Corbis; **5** (bl) ©Underwood Archives; **5** (bl) ullstein bild/ The Granger Collection; **5** (bl) Comstock/ Fotosearch; **6** (bl) ©George Ancona; **6** (br) ©George Ancona; **6** (tl) ©George Ancona; **8** ©PatrikOntkovic/Shutterstock; **9** ©Pressmaster/ Shutterstock; **10** © Ariel Skelley/CORBIS; **10** (b) © Ariel Skelley/CORBIS; **10** (tl) © Rommel/ Masterfile; **10** (tc) ©Colin Hogan/Alamy; **11** (tl) ©Bob Krist/Corbis; **11** (tr) Ariel Skelley/ CORBIS; **11** (br) ©Paul Austring Photography/ First Light/Getty Images; **11** (bl) ©Dirk Anschutz/Stone/Getty Images; **13** ©Brand X Pictures/Getty Images; **14** © Rommel/Masterfile; **15** (t) © Rommel/Masterfile; **26** © Rommel/ Masterfile; **27** © Rommel/Masterfile; **28** Ryan McVey/Photodisc/Getty Images; **29** © Rommel/ Masterfile; **30** © Heide Benser/Corbis; **30** ©Colin Hogan/Alamy; **32** ©Colin Hogan/Alamy; **32** ©Colin Hogan/Alamy; **33** (tl) © Rommel/ Masterfile; **33** ©Colin Hogan/Alamy; **34** (cl) © Photodisc / Alamy; **34** (bl) ©Juniors Bildarchiv/ Alamy; **35** (tl) © Julian Winslow/Corbis; **35** (bl) ©Rachel Watson/Stone/Getty Images; **35** (cr) © Look Photography/Beateworks/Corbis; **35** (bl) © Patrick Bennett/CORBIS; **35** Corbis; **38** (br) © Nancy G Fire Photography, Nancy Greifenhagen/Alamy Images; **38** (t) ©Amy Etra/ PhotoEdit; **38** (tc) © Douglas Keister/Corbis; **39** (cr) ©Jupiter Images/Comstock Images/Alamy; **39** (tr) ©Thomas Barwick/Riser/Getty Images; **39** (tl) ©Sascha Pflaeging/Riser/Getty Images; **39** (cl) ©Richard Hutchings/PhotoEdit; **40** Corbis; **55** Ryan McGinnis/Flickr/Getty Images; **57** Bananastock/Jupiterimages/Getty Images; **58** (c) © Douglas Keister/Corbis; **58** © Douglas Keister/ Corbis; **60** (tr) ©comstock/Getty Images; **60** (c) ©Photodisc/Don Farrall, Lightworks Studio/ Getty Images; **60** (cr) © Authors Image / Alamy; **60** (tl) © David Young-Wolff / PhotoEdit; **60** (bl) © matthiasengelien.com/Alamy; **61** ©Kenneth Langford/Corbis; **61** (b) ©GlowImages/Alamy; **61** © Douglas Keister/Corbis; **66** (c) © Michael

California Common Core State Standards for English Language Arts

LITERATURE

Key Ideas and Details

RL.1.1	Ask and answer questions about key details in a text.
RL.1.2	Retell stories, including key details, and demonstrate understanding of their central message or lesson.
RL.1.3	Describe characters, settings, and major events in a story, using key details.

Craft and Structure

RL.1.4	Identify words and phrases in stories or poems that suggest feelings or appeal to the senses. **(See grade 1 Language standards 4–6 for additional expectations.) CA**
RL.1.5	Explain major differences between books that tell stories and books that give information, drawing on a wide reading of a range of text types.
RL.1.6	Identify who is telling the story at various points in a text.

Integration of Knowledge and Ideas

RL.1.7	Use illustrations and details in a story to describe its characters, setting, or events.
RL.1.8	(Not applicable to literature)
RL.1.9	Compare and contrast the adventures and experiences of characters in stories.

Range of Reading and Level of Text Complexity

RL.1.10a	With prompting and support, read prose and poetry of appropriate complexity for grade 1. **Activate prior knowledge related to the information and events in a text. CA**
RL.1.10b	With prompting and support, read prose and poetry of appropriate complexity for grade 1. **Confirm predictions about what will happen next in a text. CA**

INFORMATIONAL TEXT

Key Ideas and Details

RI.1.1	Ask and answer questions about key details in a text.
RI.1.2	Identify the main topic and retell key details of a text.
RI.1.3	Describe the connection between two individuals, events, ideas, or pieces of information in a text.

Craft and Structure

RI.1.4	Ask and answer questions to help determine or clarify the meaning of words and phrases in a text. **(See grade 1 Language standards 4–6 for additional expectations.) CA**
RI.1.5	Know and use various text **structures (e.g., sequence) and text** features (e.g., headings, tables of contents, glossaries, electronic menus, icons) to locate key facts or information in a text. **CA**
RI.1.6	Distinguish between information provided by pictures or other illustrations and information provided by the words in a text.

Integration of Knowledge and Ideas	
RI.1.7	Use the illustrations and details in a text to describe its key ideas.
RI.1.8	Identify the reasons an author gives to support points in a text.
RI.1.9	Identify basic similarities in and differences between two texts on the same topic (e.g., in illustrations, descriptions, or procedures).

Range of Reading and Level of Text Complexity	
RI.1.10a	With prompting and support, read informational texts appropriately complex for grade 1. **Activate prior knowledge related to the information and events in a text. CA**
RI.1.10b	With prompting and support, read informational texts appropriately complex for grade 1. **Confirm predictions about what will happen next in a text. CA**

FOUNDATIONAL SKILLS

Print Concepts	
RF.1.1a	Demonstrate understanding of the organization and basic features of print. Recognize the distinguishing features of a sentence (e.g., first word, capitalization, ending punctuation).

Phonological Awareness	
RF.1.2a	Demonstrate understanding of spoken words, syllables, and sounds (phonemes). Distinguish long from short vowel sounds in spoken single-syllable words.
RF.1.2b	Demonstrate understanding of spoken words, syllables, and sounds (phonemes). Orally produce single-syllable words by blending sounds (phonemes), including consonant blends.
RF.1.2c	Demonstrate understanding of spoken words, syllables, and sounds (phonemes). Isolate and pronounce initial, medial vowel, and final sounds (phonemes) in spoken single-syllable words.
RF.1.2d	Demonstrate understanding of spoken words, syllables, and sounds (phonemes). Segment spoken single-syllable words into their complete sequence of individual sounds (phonemes).

Phonics and Word Recognition	
RF.1.3a	Know and apply grade-level phonics and word analysis skills in decoding words **both in isolation and in text. CA** Know the spelling-sound correspondences for common consonant digraphs.
RF.1.3b	Know and apply grade-level phonics and word analysis skills in decoding words **both in isolation and in text. CA** Decode regularly spelled one-syllable words.
RF.1.3c	Know and apply grade-level phonics and word analysis skills in decoding words **both in isolation and in text. CA** Know final -e and common vowel team conventions for representing long vowel sounds.

RF.1.3d	Know and apply grade-level phonics and word analysis skills in decoding words **both in isolation and in text. CA** Use knowledge that every syllable must have a vowel sound to determine the number of syllables in a printed word.
RF.1.3e	Know and apply grade-level phonics and word analysis skills in decoding words **both in isolation and in text. CA** Decode two-syllable words following basic patterns by breaking the words into syllables.
RF.1.3f	Know and apply grade-level phonics and word analysis skills in decoding words **both in isolation and in text. CA** Read words with inflectional endings.
RF.1.3g	Know and apply grade-level phonics and word analysis skills in decoding words **both in isolation and in text. CA** Recognize and read grade-appropriate irregularly spelled words.
Fluency	
RF.1.4a	Read with sufficient accuracy and fluency to support comprehension. Read on-level text with purpose and understanding.
RF.1.4b	Read with sufficient accuracy and fluency to support comprehension. Read on-level text orally with accuracy, appropriate rate, and expression on successive readings.
RF.1.4c	Read with sufficient accuracy and fluency to support comprehension. Use context to confirm or self-correct word recognition and understanding, rereading as necessary.
WRITING	
Text Types and Purposes	
W.1.1	Write opinion pieces in which they introduce the topic or name the book they are writing about, state an opinion, supply a reason for the opinion, and provide some sense of closure.
W.1.2	Write informative/explanatory texts in which they name a topic, supply some facts about the topic, and provide some sense of closure.
W.1.3	Write narratives in which they recount two or more appropriately sequenced events, include some details regarding what happened, use temporal words to signal event order, and provide some sense of closure.
Production and Distribution of Writing	
W.1.4	(Begins in grade 2) **CA**
W.1.5	With guidance and support from adults, focus on a topic, respond to questions and suggestions from peers, and add details to strengthen writing as needed.
W.1.6	With guidance and support from adults, use a variety of digital tools to produce and publish writing, including in collaboration with peers.

Research to Build and Present Knowledge	
W.1.7	Participate in shared research and writing projects (e.g., explore a number of "how-to" books on a given topic and use them to write a sequence of instructions).
W.1.8	With guidance and support from adults, recall information from experiences or gather information from provided sources to answer a question.
W.1.9	(Begins in grade 4)
Range of Writing	
W.1.10	(Begins in grade 2) **CA**
SPEAKING AND LISTENING	
Comprehension and Collaboration	
SL.1.1a	Participate in collaborative conversations with diverse partners about *grade 1 topics and texts* with peers and adults in small and larger groups. Follow agreed-upon rules for discussions (e.g., listening to others with care, speaking one at a time about the topics and texts under discussion).
SL.1.1b	Participate in collaborative conversations with diverse partners about *grade 1 topics and texts* with peers and adults in small and larger groups. Build on others' talk in conversations by responding to the comments of others through multiple exchanges.
SL.1.1c	Participate in collaborative conversations with diverse partners about *grade 1 topics and texts* with peers and adults in small and larger groups. Ask questions to clear up any confusion about the topics and texts under discussion.
SL.1.2a	Ask and answer questions about key details in a text read aloud or information presented orally or through other media. **Give, restate, and follow simple two-step directions. CA**
SL.1.3	Ask and answer questions about what a speaker says in order to gather additional information or clarify something that is not understood.
Presentation of Knowledge and Ideas	
SL.1.4a	Describe people, places, things, and events with relevant details, expressing ideas and feelings clearly. **Memorize and recite poems, rhymes, and songs with expression. CA**
SL.1.5	Add drawings or other visual displays to descriptions when appropriate to clarify ideas, thoughts, and feelings.
SL.1.6	Produce complete sentences when appropriate to task and situation. (See grade 1 Language standards 1 and 3 for specific expectations.)

LANGUAGE	
Conventions of Standard English	
L.1.1a	Demonstrate command of the conventions of standard English grammar and usage when writing or speaking. Print all upper- and lowercase letters.
L.1.1b	Demonstrate command of the conventions of standard English grammar and usage when writing or speaking. Use common, proper, and possessive nouns.
L.1.1c	Demonstrate command of the conventions of standard English grammar and usage when writing or speaking. Use singular and plural nouns with matching verbs in basic sentences (e.g., *He hops*; *We hop*).
L.1.1d	Demonstrate command of the conventions of standard English grammar and usage when writing or speaking. Use personal **(subject, object)**, possessive, and indefinite pronouns (e.g., *I, me, my*; *they, them, their*; *anyone, everything*). **CA**
L.1.1e	Demonstrate command of the conventions of standard English grammar and usage when writing or speaking. Use verbs to convey a sense of past, present, and future (e.g., Y*esterday I walked home*; *Today I walk home*; *Tomorrow I will walk home*).
L.1.1f	Demonstrate command of the conventions of standard English grammar and usage when writing or speaking. Use frequently occurring adjectives.
L.1.1g	Demonstrate command of the conventions of standard English grammar and usage when writing or speaking. Use frequently occurring conjunctions (e.g., *and, but, or, so, because*).
L.1.1h	Demonstrate command of the conventions of standard English grammar and usage when writing or speaking. Use determiners (e.g., articles, demonstratives).
L.1.1i	Demonstrate command of the conventions of standard English grammar and usage when writing or speaking. Use frequently occurring prepositions (e.g., *during, beyond, toward*).
L.1.1j	Demonstrate command of the conventions of standard English grammar and usage when writing or speaking. Produce and expand complete simple and compound declarative, interrogative, imperative, and exclamatory sentences in response to prompts.

L.1.2a	Demonstrate command of the conventions of standard English capitalization, punctuation, and spelling when writing.
	Capitalize dates and names of people.
L.1.2b	Demonstrate command of the conventions of standard English capitalization, punctuation, and spelling when writing.
	Use end punctuation for sentences.
L.1.2c	Demonstrate command of the conventions of standard English capitalization, punctuation, and spelling when writing.
	Use commas in dates and to separate single words in a series.
L.1.2d	Demonstrate command of the conventions of standard English capitalization, punctuation, and spelling when writing.
	Use conventional spelling for words with common spelling patterns and for frequently occurring irregular words.
L.1.2e	Demonstrate command of the conventions of standard English capitalization, punctuation, and spelling when writing.
	Spell untaught words phonetically, drawing on phonemic awareness and spelling conventions.
Knowledge of Language	
L.1.3	(Begins in grade 2)
Vocabulary Acquisitions and Use	
L.1.4a	Determine or clarify the meaning of unknown and multiple-meaning words and phrases based on *grade 1 reading and content*, choosing flexibly from an array of strategies.
	Use sentence-level context as a clue to the meaning of a word or phrase.
L.1.4b	Determine or clarify the meaning of unknown and multiple-meaning words and phrases based on *grade 1 reading and content*, choosing flexibly from an array of strategies.
	Use frequently occurring affixes as a clue to the meaning of a word.
L.1.4c	Determine or clarify the meaning of unknown and multiple-meaning words and phrases based on grade 1 reading and content, choosing flexibly from an array of strategies.
	Identify frequently occurring root words (e.g., *look*) and their inflectional forms (e.g., *looks, looked, looking*).
L.1.5a	With guidance and support from adults, demonstrate understanding of word relationships and nuances in word meanings.
	Sort words into categories (e.g., colors, clothing) to gain a sense of the concepts the categories represent.
L.1.5b	With guidance and support from adults, demonstrate understanding of word relationships and nuances in word meanings.
	Define words by category and by one or more key attributes (e.g., a *duck* is a bird that swims; a *tiger* is a large cat with stripes).

L.1.5c	With guidance and support from adults, demonstrate understanding of word relationships and nuances in word meanings.
	Identify real-life connections between words and their use (e.g., note places at home that are *cozy*).
L.1.5d	With guidance and support from adults, demonstrate understanding of word relationships and nuances in word meanings.
	Distinguish shades of meaning among verbs differing in manner (e.g., *look, peek, glance, stare, glare, scowl*) and adjectives differing in intensity (e.g., *large, gigantic*) by defining or choosing them or by acting out the meanings.
L.1.6	Use words and phrases acquired through conversations, reading and being read to, and responding to texts, including using frequently occurring conjunctions to signal simple relationships (e.g., *because*).

California English Language Development Standards

PART I: INTERACTING IN MEANINGFUL WAYS
A. COLLABORATIVE
1. Exchanging information and ideas
ELD.PI.1.1	**Emerging** Contribute to conversations and express ideas by asking and answering *yes-no* and *wh-* questions and responding using gestures, words, and simple phrases.
	Expanding Contribute to class, group, and partner discussions by listening attentively, following turn-taking rules, and asking and answering questions.
	Bridging Contribute to class, group, and partner discussions by listening attentively, following turn-taking rules, and asking and answering questions.
2. Interacting via written English
ELD.PI.1.2	**Emerging** Collaborate with teacher and peers on joint writing projects of short informational and literary texts, using technology where appropriate for publishing, graphics, etc.
	Expanding Collaborate with peers on joint writing projects of longer informational and literary texts, using technology where appropriate for publishing, graphics, etc.
	Bridging Collaborate with peers on joint writing projects of longer informational and literary texts, using technology where appropriate for publishing, graphics, etc.
3. Offering opinions
ELD.PI.1.3	**Emerging** Offer opinions and ideas in conversations using a small set of learned phrases (e.g., *I think X.*), as well as open responses in order to gain and/or hold the floor.
	Expanding Offer opinions and negotiate with others in conversations using an expanded set of learned phrases (e.g., *I think/don't think X. I agree with X.*), as well as open responses in order to gain and/or hold the floor, elaborate on an idea, etc.
	Bridging Offer opinions and negotiate with others in conversations using an expanded set of learned phrases (e.g., *I think/don't think X. I agree with X.*), and open responses in order to gain and/or hold the floor, elaborate on an idea, provide different opinions, etc.

4. Adapting language choices	
ELD.PI.1.4	No standard for grade 1.

5. Listening actively	
ELD.PI.1.5	**Emerging** Demonstrate active listening to read-alouds and oral presentations by asking and answering *yes-no* and *wh-* questions with oral sentence frames and substantial prompting and support. **Expanding** Demonstrate active listening to read-alouds and oral presentations by asking and answering questions with oral sentence frames and occasional prompting and support. **Bridging** Demonstrate active listening to read-alouds and oral presentations by asking and answering detailed questions with minimal prompting and light support.

6. Reading/viewing closely	
ELD.PI.1.6	**Emerging** Describe ideas, phenomena (e.g., plant life cycle), and text elements (e.g., characters) based on understanding of a select set of grade-level texts and viewing of multimedia with substantial support. **Expanding** Describe ideas, phenomena (e.g., how earthworms eat), and text elements (e.g., setting, main idea) in greater detail based on understanding of a variety of grade-level texts and viewing of multimedia with moderate support. **Bridging** Describe ideas, phenomena (e.g., erosion), and text elements (e.g., central message, character traits) using key details based on understanding of a variety of grade-level texts and viewing of multimedia with light support.

7. Evaluating language choices	
ELD.PI.1.7	**Emerging** Describe the language writers or speakers use to present an idea (e.g., the words and phrases used to describe a character) with prompting and substantial support. **Expanding** Describe the language writers or speakers use to present or support an idea (e.g., the adjectives used to describe people and places) with prompting and moderate support. **Bridging** Describe the language writers or speakers use to present or support an idea (e.g., the author's choice of vocabulary to portray characters, places, or real people) with prompting and light support.

8. Analyzing language choices	
ELD.PI.1.8	**Emerging** Distinguish how two different frequently used words (e.g., *large* versus *small*) produce a different effect on the audience. **Expanding** Distinguish how two different words with similar meaning (e.g., *large* versus *enormous*) produce shades of meaning and a different effect on the audience. **Bridging** Distinguish how multiple different words with similar meaning (e.g., *big, large, huge, enormous, gigantic*) produce shades of meaning and a different effect on the audience.

C. PRODUCTIVE	
9. Presenting	
ELD.PI.1.9	**Emerging** Plan and deliver very brief oral presentations (e.g., show and tell, describing a picture). **Expanding** Plan and deliver brief oral presentations on a variety of topics (e.g., show and tell, author's chair, recounting an experience, describing an animal, etc.). **Bridging** Plan and deliver longer oral presentations on a variety of topics in a variety of content areas (e.g., retelling a story, describing a science experiment).
10. Writing	
ELD.PI.1.10	**Emerging** Write very short literary texts (e.g., story) and informational texts (e.g., a description of an insect) using familiar vocabulary collaboratively with an adult (e.g., joint construction of texts), with peers, and sometimes independently. **Expanding** Write short literary texts (e.g., a story) and informational texts (e.g., an informative text on the life cycle of an insect) collaboratively with an adult (e.g., joint construction of texts), with peers, and with increasing independence. **Bridging** Write longer literary texts (e.g., a story) and informational texts (e.g., an informative text on the life cycle of insects) collaboratively with an adult (e.g., joint construction), with peers, and independently.
11. Supporting opinions	
ELD.PI.1.11	**Emerging** Offer opinions and provide good reasons (e.g., *My favorite book is X because X.*) referring to the text or to relevant background knowledge. **Expanding** Offer opinions and provide good reasons and some textual evidence or relevant background knowledge (e.g., paraphrased examples from text or knowledge of content). **Bridging** Offer opinions and provide good reasons with detailed textual evidence or relevant background knowledge (e.g., specific examples from text or knowledge of content).
12. Selecting language resources	
ELD.PI.1.12a	**Emerging** Retell texts and recount experiences, using key words. **Expanding** Retell texts and recount experiences, using complete sentences and key words. **Bridging** Retell texts and recount experiences, using increasingly detailed complete sentences and key words.
ELD.PI.1.12b	**Emerging** Use a select number of general academic and domain-specific words to add detail (e.g., adding the word *scrumptious* to describe a favorite food, using the word *thorax* to refer to insect anatomy) while speaking and writing. **Expanding** Use a growing number of general academic and domain-specific words in order to add detail, create an effect (e.g., using the word *suddenly* to signal a change), or create shades of meaning (e.g., *prance* versus *walk*) while speaking and writing. **Bridging** Use a wide variety of general academic and domain-specific words, synonyms, antonyms, and non-literal language (e.g., The dog was *as big as a house.*) to create an effect, precision, and shades of meaning while speaking and writing.

PART II: LEARNING ABOUT HOW ENGLISH WORKS
A. STRUCTURING COHESIVE TEXTS

1. Understanding text structure	
ELD.PII.1.1	**Emerging** Apply understanding of how text types are organized (e.g., how a story is organized by a sequence of events) to comprehending texts and composing basic texts with substantial support (e.g., using drawings, through joint construction with a peer or teacher) to comprehending texts and writing texts in shared language activities guided by the teacher, with peers, and sometimes independently.
	Expanding Apply understanding of how different text types are organized to express ideas (e.g., how a story is organized sequentially with predictable stages versus how an informative text is organized by topic and details) to comprehending texts and writing texts in shared language activities guided by the teacher and with increasing independence.
	Bridging Apply understanding of how different text types are organized predictably to express ideas (e.g., how a story is organized versus an informative/explanatory text versus an opinion text) to comprehending texts and writing texts in shared language activities guided by the teacher and independently.

2. Understanding cohesion	
ELD.PII.1.2	**Emerging** Apply basic understanding of how ideas, events, or reasons are linked throughout a text using more everyday connecting words or phrases (e.g., *one day*, *after*, *then*) to comprehending texts and writing texts in shared language activities guided by the teacher, with peers, and sometimes independently.
	Expanding Apply understanding of how ideas, events, or reasons are linked throughout a text using a growing number of connecting words or phrases (e.g., *a long time ago*, *suddenly*) to comprehending texts and writing texts in shared language activities guided by the teacher and with increasing independence.
	Bridging Apply understanding of how ideas, events, or reasons are linked throughout a text using a variety of connecting words or phrases (e.g., *for example*, *after that*, *first/second/third*) to comprehending texts and writing texts in shared language activities guided by the teacher and independently.

B. EXPANDING & ENRICHING IDEAS	
3. Using verbs and verb phrases	
ELD.PII.1.3a	**Emerging** Use frequently used verbs (e.g., go, eat, run) and verb types (e.g., doing, saying, being/ having, thinking/feeling) in shared language activities guided by the teacher and sometimes independently. **Expanding** Use a growing number of verbs and verb types (e.g., doing, saying, being/having, thinking/feeling) in shared language activities guided by the teacher and with increasing independence. **Bridging** Use a wide variety of verbs and verb types (e.g., doing, saying, being/having, thinking/ feeling) in shared language activities guided by the teacher and independently.
ELD.PII.1.3b	**Emerging** Use simple verb tenses appropriate for the text type and discipline to convey time (e.g., simple past for recounting an experience) in shared language activities guided by the teacher and sometimes independently. **Expanding** Use a growing number of verb tenses appropriate for the text type and discipline to convey time (e.g., simple past tense for retelling, simple present for a science description) in shared language activities guided by the teacher and with increasing independence. **Bridging** Use a wide variety of verb tenses appropriate for the text type and discipline to convey time (e.g., simple present for a science description, simple future to predict) in shared language activities guided by the teacher and independently.
4. Using nouns and noun phrases	
ELD.PII.1.4	**Emerging** Expand noun phrases in simple ways (e.g., adding a familiar adjective to describe a noun) in order to enrich the meaning of sentences and add details about ideas, people, things, etc., in shared language activities guided by the teacher and sometimes independently. **Expanding** Expand noun phrases in a growing number of ways (e.g., adding a newly learned adjective to a noun) in order to enrich the meaning of sentences and add details about ideas, people, things, etc., in shared language activities guided by the teacher and with increasing independence. **Bridging** Expand noun phrases in a wide variety of ways (e.g., adding a variety of adjectives to noun phrases) in order to enrich the meaning of phrases/sentences and add details about ideas, people, things, etc., in shared language activities guided by the teacher and independently.
5. Modifying to add details	
ELD.PII.1.5	**Emerging** Expand sentences with frequently used prepositional phrases (such as *in the house*, *on the boat*) to provide details (e.g., time, manner, place, cause) about a familiar activity or process in shared language activities guided by the teacher and sometimes independently. **Expanding** Expand sentences with prepositional phrases to provide details (e.g., time, manner, place, cause) about a familiar or new activity or process in shared language activities guided by the teacher and with increasing independence. **Bridging** Expand simple and compound sentences with prepositional phrases to provide details (e.g., time, manner, place, cause) in shared language activities guided by the teacher and independently.

C. CONNECTING & CONDENSING IDEAS	
6. Connecting ideas	
ELD.PII.1.6	**Emerging** Combine clauses in a few basic ways to make connections between and to join ideas (e.g., creating compound sentences using *and, but, so*) in shared language activities guided by the teacher and sometimes independently. **Expanding** Combine clauses in an increasing variety of ways to make connections between and to join ideas, for example, to express cause/effect (e.g., *She jumped because the dog barked.*), in shared language activities guided by the teacher and with increasing independence. **Bridging** Combine clauses in a wide variety of ways (e.g., rearranging complete, simple-to-form compound sentences) to make connections between and to join ideas (e.g., *The boy was hungry. The boy ate a sandwich. -> The boy was hungry <u>so</u> he ate a sandwich.*) in shared language activities guided by the teacher and independently.
7. Condensing ideas	
ELD.PII.1.7	**Emerging** Condense clauses in simple ways (e.g., changing: *I like blue. I like red. I like purple -> I like blue, red, and purple.*) to create precise and detailed sentences in shared language activities guided by the teacher and sometimes independently. **Expanding** Condense clauses in a growing number of ways (e.g., through embedded clauses as in, *She's a doctor. She saved the animals. -> She's the doctor who saved the animals.*) to create precise and detailed sentences in shared language activities guided by the teacher and with increasing independence. **Bridging** Condense clauses in a variety of ways (e.g., through embedded clauses and other condensing, for example, through embedded clauses as in *She's a doctor. She's amazing. She saved the animals. -> She's the amazing doctor who saved the animals.*) to create precise and detailed sentences in shared language activities guided by the teacher and independently.
Part III: USING FOUNDATIONAL LITERACY SKILLS	
Foundational Literacy Skills (See Appendix A-Grade One):	
ELD.PIII.1	Literacy in an Alphabetic Writing System • Print concepts • Phonological awareness • Phonics & word recognition • Fluency